NEW Spirals ... ICTION

CW01651727

The Biz

Helen Lowerson

First published in 2001 by:
Nelson Thornes Ltd
Delta Place
27 Bath Road
CHELTENHAM
GL53 7TH
United Kingdom

01 02 03 04 05 / 10 9 8 7 6 5 4 3 2 1

A catalogue record for this book is available from the British Library.

ISBN 0-7487-6062-8

Cover artwork by Martin Berry
Typeset by Tech-Set Ltd, Gateshead
Printed and bound in Great Britain by Martins The Printers Ltd, Berwick upon Tweed

1

'We want The Biz! We want The Biz!'

The crowd stamped and yelled for the band. The stage was dark.

'We want The Biz!'

A sudden drumbeat thudded from the stage. A guitar note hummed and the whole stage lit up. The crowd went wild, yelling, cheering and jumping about madly.

Emma's heart thudded. Her blue eyes shone with excitement. She cheered and yelled with the rest. Her best friend Mand was beside her, waving her hands in the air and screaming. On stage, The Biz was playing the opening song.

Emma gazed up at the singer as he sang. She sang every word with him. The songs were about her life, about her hopes and dreams. Her eyes never left the singer as he danced across the stage.

The first time Emma had seen The Biz she had fallen in love with their music. She had also fallen madly in love with Rob, the singer. Mand was in love with Rob too and the girls never missed a show.

'He's boss!' Mand said.

'He must work out,' Emma said. 'He's got such lush muscles.'

'Those eyes!' Mand said. 'The colour of chocolate . . .'

'I'd love to run my fingers through his hair,' Emma said dreamily.

'It's a bit short, isn't it?' Mand said.

Emma just shook her head. She could almost feel the soft, short spikes against her palm.

'It's not that I think it's too short,' Mand didn't want Emma to think she didn't like Rob. 'It makes him look so cute like that. Just a bit short for running your fingers through.'

Emma shrugged. Maybe one day she'd find out. She and Mand always stood at the front of the stage at gigs. They knew he'd seen them. Sometimes he'd sing straight at them. That would make their knees go weak and start them screaming.

Emma and Mand swayed together in time with the music. They sang the words with the band. Their eyes never left the singer's face.

'I'll love you all my life, 'cos I need you so! No one could love you more, 'cos I want you so!'

Emma could feel tears on her cheeks. She hoped Rob could hear her singing to him. She hoped when he closed his eyes and sang it was so he would see only her.

A sudden clatter on the drums changed the mood. The band began a fast song. Rob jumped about the stage. The rest of the band concentrated on playing the rapid beat.

Emma sobbed back a last tear and began to jump to the music. She and Mand yelled with the rest of the crowd.

For the next hour the girls sang and danced as the band played their best songs. They didn't notice the people pushing beside and behind them. They watched only Rob as he ran about the stage. They didn't even notice the other three band members. The girls were only there for Rob.

At last the band left the stage and the lights came on in the hall. Emma and Mand had to wait as the crowds left. They felt dizzy and breathless after the show.

'Wasn't he fab tonight?' Mand said.

'He was singing right to me,' Emma sighed.

Mand snorted. 'Huh! Like when? He didn't even see you.'

Emma just shrugged. 'Didn't hear him asking you out,' she said.

'Do you think they still have the "Club Land" CD?' Mand asked, changing the subject.

The girls were best friends. They didn't want to fall out. Even over a hunk like Rob.

'If we're quick,' Emma grabbed Mand's arm. 'Come on!'

She dragged Mand through the last few people going out of the door. The small lobby was full of CDs, T-shirts, posters, caps and badges for sale. Everything had 'The Biz' on it and most things had a picture of the band too.

Mand went straight to the box of CDs. She soon found the one she wanted. Emma looked through a pile of T-shirts. She counted her money slowly. If they walked home, she could buy a new T-shirt with a photo of Rob on the front.

Mand came up just as Emma had made up her mind.

'Can you lend me the bus fare,' Mand asked, 'or shall we walk?'

Emma smiled at her friend. 'I'll just pay for this T-shirt. Then we'll start walking.'

The friends walked home arm in arm. Mand couldn't wait to listen to her CD.

'If I put on my headphones, I can listen to it in bed. Mum will think I've gone to sleep,' she giggled. 'She hates The Biz. Says they can't sing or play. What would she know?'

Emma smiled. 'Music wasn't like that when she was young, I bet!'

They laughed. Their parents didn't like the girls going to every gig. A lot of their school friends went and the gigs were all at local halls, so they put up with it. Emma and Mand didn't care what their parents thought. They would do anything to see The Biz play.

'What are you going to do with your T-shirt, Emma? Isn't it a bit big for you?'

'I'm going to wear it as a nightshirt,' Emma smiled to herself. 'Then I can curl up in bed with my arms round Rob all night.'

'It's the closest you'll get,' Mand said. 'Let's have a look at it then.'

As Emma pulled the T-shirt from the bag, a slip of paper fell out. Mand caught it before it blew away.

'Oh my God!' her eyes shone as she read. 'They're playing City Hall next month! It'll be so big! Tickets go on sale next week. We have to go.'

Emma grabbed the slip from Mand and read it. This was going to be great. The Biz needed a big break. And this was it. Emma was sure of it.

'Thank goodness I'm babysitting tomorrow night,' Emma said. 'I bet the tickets won't be cheap.'

'About time we got in on the guest list,' Mand muttered.

'I'll put in a good word for you sometime,' Emma joked.

The girls rushed home, laughing. They would have to be busy to earn the money for the tickets, but this was one gig they were not going to miss.

2

As the bus came round the corner, Emma started to run. The leg of her jeans was damp and it clung to her knee. Emma reached the bus stop just as the bus drew to a halt. Panting, she climbed on and paid her fare. Mand was sitting at the back, grinning at her.

'What kept you?'

Emma took some deep breaths before she could reply. 'Had to wash the car again. Dad gave me the money last week so I could buy the ticket. Wouldn't let me go until I'd finished.'

Over the last few weeks, Emma and Mand had done every job they could find. They had washed cars and done extra chores round the house. Mand had babysat for her cousin every Saturday night that month. It had been hard work, but they had managed to get tickets to see The Biz at City Hall.

'All set then?' Mand asked.

Emma nodded. Her face showed her excitement. She wore jeans and a white strappy top. Her long blonde hair was held in a loose ponytail. She pulled out the band and shook her hair. It shone in the sunlight. Mand felt the usual stab of jealousy. Her own hair was short, dark and curly. She wished she had hair like Emma's.

'Shall we get a McDonald's on the way?' Emma asked.

'Yeah,' Mand agreed. 'It'll be a long wait.'

'Ages,' Emma sighed. 'I wish it had already started. I can't wait to hear them in a proper hall.'

'I wonder what Rob will wear. Do you think he'll have something new?'

Emma nodded dreamily. 'Black leather trousers.'

'And?'

Emma smiled wickedly. 'And nothing.'

Mand smiled too. The girls fell silent as they imagined Rob in his stage gear.

The street outside the City Hall wasn't busy. A few shoppers hurried past on their way to more shops or to catch an early bus home. The girls settled themselves at the door and ate their McDonald's. It was late summer and the sun was still warm. Emma looked at her watch.

'Only another four hours until the doors open,' she told Mand.

Mand nodded, her mouth full of chips.

'Do we really need to be here so early?' Emma asked.

'We've got to be at the front. We couldn't miss that. Not for their first big gig.'

Emma pushed a small stone with the toe of her boot. 'I bet the band's not even here yet,' she sighed.

Mand grabbed her arm, eyes gleaming. 'Maybe we'll see them arrive!'

Emma cheered up. 'Yes! And they'll see us.'

By seven o'clock, both girls were beginning to get cold and bored. A few people had begun to drift into a queue behind them. Emma wrapped her jacket round her. Mand's stomach rumbled.

'Do you think there'll be a burger stall inside?' she asked.

Emma put a friendly arm round her shoulder. 'No, love, but if you're a good girl, mummy will buy you an ice cream at the break.'

Mand pushed Emma's arm off. 'Ha, ha!' Her tummy growled again. 'I suppose we can get some chips on the way home.'

Emma glanced behind her. More people had joined the queue. The girls had spent all afternoon waiting. Now it seemed time well spent. Mand followed her friend's gaze.

'We could have got here a *bit* later than three o'clock,' she muttered.

'Oh, come on!' Emma hugged her friend. 'We're going to see The Biz at the City Hall. We're going to be right at the very front by the stage. Rob will see me – and you – just where we always are. It's going to be the best gig ever!'

The doors rattled as they were unlocked. The crowd began to push forward. Emma and Mand rushed to be first in. They barely stopped to show their tickets. They ran right to the front by the stage.

Emma looked round. The stage curtain was closed but she could tell that the stage was much bigger than any stage the band had played on before. It was higher too. The floor of the hall had a carpet and the rows of seats had dark blue padding on them.

'Wow! Dead posh.' Emma felt knots of excitement in her tummy. 'Keep my space. I'm going to the loo.'

She darted off. She got to the Ladies just as the queue was starting. After she'd been to the loo, she touched up her make-up and brushed her hair. She wanted Rob to see her looking special. It was a special night.

The hall had really filled up while she had been away. She had to push through the crowd to get back to Mand. Some people glared and didn't give way. Emma had to push and squeeze through any gap she could find.

Mand checked her watch. 'Half an hour till they start. Reckon I'd better go too. Don't want to miss any of the action!'

Mand quickly disappeared into the crowd. Everyone wanted to be in the space between the chairs and the stage. The Biz played good dance music. No one wanted to be sitting.

Emma began to feel hot. She wriggled out of her jacket. There was hardly any room to move. Mand finally managed to push back in. Emma felt even more crushed with her friend beside her.

Mand was full of chat. She told Emma about the people they knew who were in seats six rows back.

'They'll be so cross when they find out we were right at the front!'

Emma couldn't reply. Her head felt thick. Mand seemed to be getting fainter. She felt herself begin to sway. She yawned, but didn't feel tired. The house lights dimmed and a murmur of excitement swept through the crowd.

Emma looked up to the stage. Everything swam in front of her. The stage seemed to go fuzzy. She clutched at arms and legs as she fell. She thought she heard Mand call her name.

Moments later, she was lifted up as two first aiders carried her through the crowd. She saw the stage curtain swing open. The stage burst into light and The Biz stormed into their first song.

'No!' Emma tried to struggle, but her head was still spinning and her arms and legs felt heavy.

She was put on a bed in the first aid room backstage. Kind faces checked her over. Soft voices told her to relax, that she was going to be OK. Emma turned her tear-streaked face to the wall. All she could hear was the dull thudding of The Biz's first big gig through the walls.

3

The cheering grew very loud, even in the small first aid room backstage. Every now and then Emma sniffed back a tear as she sat, a half-empty mug of sweet tea in her hand.

The first aiders had been kind. When Emma had not calmed down, they had just sat with her. She had sobbed for nearly an hour. She had cried as if her heart had broken. Now the concert was over, she had no energy left.

There was a buzz of voices outside. The cheering from the hall began to die away. People were talking about the gig as they shuffled out.

Emma stared gloomily at the dusty floor. Perhaps she could go home now. Maybe Mand would wait outside for her. She sighed deeply.

'Hi there,' a man said from the doorway.

Emma was too miserable to look up.

'Hi,' said the man again. 'I don't know your name, but we know your face. Right guys?'

'Yes,' added another voice. 'You're always at the front.'

'Where's your friend?' someone else asked.

Emma looked up and her jaw dropped. Right in front of her – so close she could touch them – was The Biz! The whole band.

'Feeling better?' Rob smiled at her.

Emma closed her mouth and swallowed hard. She smiled weakly and nodded. The four band members crowded into the small room. The first aiders smiled at Emma as they went to wait outside.

Rob dropped himself onto the bed beside her. Emma felt she might faint again. Her heart beat so fast.

'Was it you they took out? Right at the start?' he asked.

Emma nodded sadly. 'It was the crowd. Mand and me wanted to be right at the front . . .'

'Like always,' someone chipped in.

Emma felt a thrill. The band *had* noticed them. She nodded.

'There was a big crush. I fell, so they took me out here. Then they wouldn't let me back in.'

'Did you miss the whole show?' Rob asked.

'Yes,' Emma said sadly. 'Even the encores. You can't hear much back here.'

'Tell you what,' Rob took her hand. Emma held her breath. It was a dream come true. 'Our next gig is going to be bigger. And it's going to be even better. We haven't put up the ads yet. It's going to be at the Lanton Arena.'

'Wow!' Emma was thrilled. It was the biggest venue around. It would be wicked to see The Biz playing there.

'It'll be massive!' said the drummer happily.

The band whistled and whooped.

'OK!' Rob held up one hand, grinning, but his other arm was still round Emma. 'We're only the support band – this time. Give us your address and we'll arrange some tickets, maybe even some backstage passes. Put you on the guest list.'

Emma's mouth fell open again. Her eyes were wide.

'Will you?' she asked. Did he mean it?

Someone found some paper and someone else had a pen. Carefully Emma wrote down her name and address. Rob read it before folding it carefully and putting it into his back pocket.

'Well, Emma,' he stood up smiling. 'Watch the post!'

He gave her hand a gentle squeeze as the others said goodbye. They disappeared down the corridor, laughing and shouting to each other. Emma was left stunned.

She had met the band. Rob had sat beside her. He had held her hand. He had put his arm round her. He was sending her a backstage pass for the biggest concert of the year. She was on the guest list. But best of all – Rob knew her name.

As she sat trying to take it all in, Mand arrived.

'Oh Emma! What a show you missed!' she began.

Emma looked at her. Her face was shining. 'The next one will be better.'

'Yes, well, you might not faint at the next one,' Mand said, trying to cheer Emma up.

'The band are sending me tickets,' Emma blurted out, too excited to keep the news to herself any longer.

Mand looked at her as if she'd gone mad. 'What do you mean?'

'They came here, after the show. Rob sat beside me,' her voice rose with excitement. 'He held my hand and he said he'd send me tickets to their next show. At Lanton Arena!'

Emma's voice was almost a squeak, but Mand had lost all her excitement at having seen the gig. She wasn't sure whether to believe Emma or not. Maybe she was making it up because she had missed the show.

'Honest?' she asked.

''Course!' Emma said. 'Rob knows my name! I'm on the guest list.'

Mand bit her lip. She stared at her friend's tear-streaked face, now so happy. 'I'm surprised he remembered you,' she snapped. 'You look like a panda left out in the rain.'

For weeks, Emma was in a dream world. All she could think of was Rob sitting beside her holding her hand. And the promise of tickets that meant she would see him again.

Mand sulked. She kept saying how brill the band had been on stage. How the whole crowd had sung along to 'Dance With Me', Emma's favourite song. How there would never be another show like it.

But Emma didn't care. If she never heard the band play again, she would be content with her memory of meeting Rob. That was a lie, though. All she wanted was the chance to meet him again.

'His hand was so soft,' she told Mand yet again, her eyes misty with the memory. 'His teeth are so white. You wouldn't believe it! Oh, and his muscles up close . . .'

She closed her eyes to remember. Mand screwed up her face in disgust. She felt she had got the worst from that night. She had loved seeing the band on the big stage. They had played so well and everyone had got into it, dancing and singing. But if she had stayed with Emma, she would have met the band too.

At last the next concert was advertised. Rob had not sent tickets. Mand stopped being so sure Emma had met Rob. Emma stopped being so sure Rob would remember her. Tickets were selling fast and Mand wanted to go and get tickets before they sold out.

'No. Rob said he'd send me some,' Emma said firmly. She was not sure, but she clung to her dream. Her dream that Rob would hold her hand again.

'Yes, yes,' Mand muttered. 'I'm going to get myself one anyway. You can miss another gig if you like.'

'Wait just another week,' Emma pleaded.

If the tickets hadn't come by then, she would buy a ticket too. Then she would cry herself to sleep. Cry with disappointment that Rob had forgotten her.

4

Emma and Mand waited in the long line. The Arena loomed in front of them. They had never been to a concert so big before. Most of the people seemed a lot older. Secretly the girls worried that they might not be allowed in. They felt that if they spoke, it might turn out to be a dream.

'Have you got the tickets?' said Mand. Her voice was almost a whisper.

'Yes, just as I had them five minutes ago, last time you asked,' Emma hissed back.

The queue moved forward a few paces. Emma looked past the people in front.

'Still loads more to go in,' she said nervously. The crowd would be much bigger this time. She hoped she wasn't going to faint again.

'My Mum says it's dead brill inside,' Mand confided. 'She went to see some musical here.'

Emma shot Mand a dirty look. 'What's your Mum got to do with tonight? This is the biggest gig we've ever been to and you're mouthing on about your Mum.'

'OK! OK! I was only saying,' Mand huffed back.

They shuffled forward a few paces and stood in silence.

'Get the tickets out, Em,' Mand begged.

Emma rolled her eyes to the sky and sighed.

'I will, if it will stop you going on about it.' She opened her small handbag and dug about.

Mand held her breath.

'You did get tickets, didn't you?' Mand asked at last. 'You didn't just say you had to keep up your story.'

Emma looked up from her bag and glared at Mand.

'What story?' she demanded.

'About Rob sending you tickets and passes,' Mand said.

'It isn't a story,' Emma said crossly. She took two tickets and passes from her bag and waved them at her friend. 'There! Now will you relax and let's have the best night ever.'

Mand tried to hide her surprise. She had never really believed Emma had met the band. She thought she had bought the tickets herself. But when she saw the backstage passes, she knew Emma must have got them from the band. And if she *had* met the band, it might also be true that she had held Rob's hand.

As the girls shuffled forward in the queue again, Mand was getting angry. She wished she had missed the last gig and been backstage with Emma. Now that Rob had met Emma, would he even notice her? She was determined to make him.

The man on the door told them they could go backstage any time. They just had to show their passes. The girls decided to see the gig first. As The Biz were support, they would be on first.

The crowd was buzzing. Emma and Mand began to feel more excited than nervous as they found their seats.

'We aren't at the front,' Mand muttered. 'Looks as if Rob didn't fancy you much.'

'The Biz are support. Those seats are probably full of the other group's fans,' Emma replied. 'What are you moaning about, anyway? You got in for free. We'd never have found the money for the tickets. And we get to go backstage any time we like.'

Mand shrugged and looked away. It was a thrill to be at the gig, but she still felt cross. She'd missed out on meeting the band before, but she was going to make herself known this time. Emma was very pretty, but Mand knew it was the way you acted that got you noticed.

The house lights dimmed. The murmuring of the crowd grew. Any moment the gig would burst into life. Emma held her breath, her gaze fixed on the stage. Her heart pounded. She couldn't wait to see Rob again.

The curtains lifted. The stage was in darkness. The crowd fell silent. Emma peered onto the stage, but couldn't make anything out.

A single spotlight picked out the drummer as he began to beat out a slow rhythm. The guitarist joined in with gentle chords as he, too, was lit up. As the light fell on the bass player, the deep notes added to the music.

Emma held her breath and peered harder at the dark space left at the front of the stage. Rob must be there.

Suddenly she was blinking as a blaze of sparks flared up. The music changed to a fast beat. The crowd cheered.

When Emma could see properly again, the crowd and the band were leaping up and down. There was Rob, running about on the stage, mike in hand.

Mand was already on her feet, clapping her hands and singing along. Still a bit dazed from the stage explosion, Emma stood up and joined in with the song. It seemed to end all too soon. Rob introduced the band and went into the next song.

Emma swayed to the beat and sang the words she knew so well. As always, she only had eyes for Rob. He wore loose black trousers and a tight white T-shirt. His arms looked tanned and strong.

His hair was short, almost spiky. Emma wondered how it would feel against her cheek. She longed to see if his eyes were the melting chocolate brown she remembered. She was too far away to tell, but still her gaze went to his eyes.

With a jolt she realised he was staring back at her as he sang. Her cheeks went red. She felt them burning. Before she could drop her gaze, Rob winked at her. And then he was dancing across the stage.

Emma's mouth fell open. Then she smiled to herself as a tingle of excitement ran through her. It must be a good sign!

The rest of the concert passed in a haze for Emma. She sang and danced, but her mind was playing over when Rob had winked at her. Mand seemed to be lost in the music. She hadn't spoken to Emma since the gig started. Emma was happy to be left with her thoughts of Rob.

When the curtain finally went down on The Biz's set, Emma could hardly wait to go backstage. Mand didn't seem to be in too much of a hurry.

'They'll need time to come down after the gig,' she told Mand. 'Just cool it. They'll still be there in another five minutes.'

'Come on, Mand!' Emma begged. 'We have to find them first. It could take ages.'

'Well, if you're such a baby that you can't wait,' Mand sighed.

'Aren't you excited about going backstage?' Emma asked as they started to push through the crowd.

Mand shrugged. 'It'll be cool.'

They showed their passes and were told where to go. They walked through a maze of corridors. Apart from the dull thudding of music, it seemed empty backstage. At last they came to the room. They could hear laughing and talking behind the door. It was obvious it wasn't just the band inside.

Emma stood by the door. 'Should we knock?'

Mand looked at her with pity. 'It isn't the headmaster's office,' she said.

She flung open the door. Everyone in the room stopped to look. Mand walked straight over to Rob, leaving Emma hovering by the door.

'Hi. I'm Mand,' she smiled up at him through her long, dark lashes. 'Thanks for the tickets. You were *so* good on stage tonight. It was a brilliant gig.'

'Er, thanks,' said Rob, not quite sure who this girl was. 'Can I get you a drink?'

He waved his hand towards a table covered with bottles. Mand linked her arm through his and steered him towards the table, his back to the still open door. She smiled up at him.

'I think I've seen something I'd like.'

5

Emma bit her lip, unsure of what to do. Mand was laughing and talking to Rob. They still had their backs to her. She didn't know anybody else. Emma went over to get a drink. Mand glared at her.

'Let's go somewhere quieter,' Mand said to Rob.

They pushed their way through the crowd. Emma watched them go. Rob hadn't noticed her at all.

She got a Coke and looked round. Everyone was talking and having a good time. She felt like crying. Had it all been a dream? Rob had sent her tickets to the gig. Now it was as if they had never met.

Emma stared into her cup. She blinked. If she cried her make-up would look a mess. Someone put on some music. Emma didn't feel like dancing. She wished she were at home.

'Want to dance?'

Emma looked up. Her heart stopped.

In front of her stood Rob. He was smiling at her. His eyes were a melting chocolate brown. His hand was held out to her. Emma put her hand in his and he led her to join the dancing.

Emma was soon lost in Rob's eyes and the music. She saw Mand across the room. Emma looked away. Rob had seen her first. Mand had no right to be upset.

'Fancy going somewhere a bit quieter?' Rob asked.

Emma nodded. She knew Mand was watching them.

Rob led her by the hand into corridor. The music from the party was still loud. He took her into the next room. The music still thudded through the wall. There was no one to spy on them.

'Alone at last,' Emma said with a giggle.

Rob was so close. She could feel his breath on her cheek. She could almost feel his lips on hers. She gazed into his eyes, ready to melt.

Rob put his hand on her waist.

'Let me look at you,' he said softly.

Suddenly he pulled her T-shirt up. It was right over her face. Emma felt his hands grabbing at her. She pulled away, but Rob held her against him.

'Stop it! Get off me!' Emma tried to push him away.

'What's the matter?' Rob whispered. 'I know you want me to touch you.'

'No! Get off!' Emma shouted.

She twisted away from his hands. She tried to get to the door. Rob grabbed her wrist and pulled her back.

'Relax,' Rob said. 'You're going to enjoy this. They all do.'

He laughed and held her tighter. Emma screamed and kicked at him. She heard him swear. His face looked angry.

'Stop mucking me about.' He put his face up to hers. 'You've been asking for this for months.'

He kissed her. It wasn't like her dreams. It wasn't soft and sweet. It wasn't the kind of kiss she wanted. It was hard and it hurt. She could smell beer on his breath. Emma struggled. She couldn't breathe.

'What the hell is going on?'

Rob looked to the door. Emma jumped away from him. She ran to Mand, who was at the door.

'Are you all right?' she asked Emma.

Emma nodded. She was so glad to see Mand.

'You can't treat my friend like that,' Mand said.

'Let's go,' Emma said. 'I just want to go.'

'She asked for it,' Rob said angrily. 'Both of you have been asking for it. Don't start acting all sweet now.'

'I thought you were something so special,' Emma said, close to tears.

'Let's go. He's not worth wasting our time on any more,' Mand said.

The girls hugged each other as they walked down the corridor.

'Bitches. Both of you!' Rob shouted after them. 'Just a pair of bitches.'

The girls walked on without looking back.

'I'm so glad you came in when you did,' Emma said to Mand.

'I was looking for you,' Mand said. 'I wanted to be with Rob. I was angry when you left the room with him.'

'I was angry when you started chatting him up,' Emma told her.

'I thought he was so wonderful.'

Emma sighed. 'I've dreamt of kissing him for months. Now it's a bad dream.'

Mand hugged her friend.

'Tomorrow we'll take all our posters and T-shirts. We'll put them on my Dad's bonfire in the garden.'

Emma nodded. 'I want to get rid of everything. Will the CDs burn?'

'Are you mad?' said Mand. 'We'll sell those. With the money we'll go to see a film together.'

'Thanks, Mand,' Emma said.

'What for?'

'For being my friend.'